JavaScript Exercises with Data Structures and Algorithms

ISBN: 9798332253706

Copyright © 2024 by Haris Tsetsekas

Table of Contents

1. University Courses 5
2. Restaurant Reservations 7
3. Library 11
4. Contact List 17
5. Priority Todo List 21
6. Songs List 27
7. Task allocation 31
8. Word Frequencies 37
9. Syntax Checker 39
10. Maze Solver 43
11. File Indexer 49
12. Inventory with AVL Tree 53
13. Social Network 59
14. Flights 65
15. MNIST Image Comparison 71
16. HTTP Server with Caching 77
17. Auction 83

1. University Courses

Let's create a program that will handle the enrollment for university courses. Each course has one or more prerequisites, i.e. courses that must have been completed by a student in order to be able to enroll in the specific one.

Proposed Solution

First of all, we will define the class for a student in the university:

```
class Student {
  constructor(id, name, courses) {
    this.id = id;
    this.name = name;
    this.courses = courses;
  }
}
```

Listing 1-1: universityCourses.js

This class contains information about the student and the courses that have been completed successfully. The `courses` array contains the ID of the course.

Next, we define a class for the university courses:

```
class Course {
  constructor(id, name, prereqIDs) {
    this.id = id;
    this.name = name;
    this.prereqIDs = prereqIDs;
  }

  canEnroll(student) {
    for (const prereqId of this.prereqIDs) {
      if (!student.courses.includes(prereqId)) {
        return false;
      }
    }
    return true;
  }
}
```

Listing 1-2: universityCourses.js

Each course contains an array of the IDs of the prerequisite courses. The class also includes a function that finds out whether a student can enroll on a course. For each prerequisite course, this function tries to match it with a course already taken by the student.

Finally, the rest of the code:

```
const courses = [
  new Course(0, 'Intro to Programming', [-1]),
  new Course(1, 'Data Structures', [0]),
```

```js
    new Course(2, 'Algorithms', [1]),
    new Course(3, 'Database Management', [0]),
    new Course(4, 'Web Development', [0]),
    new Course(5, 'Operating Systems', [1, 2]),
    new Course(6, 'Computer Networks', [1, 5]),
    new Course(7, 'Software Engineering', [1, 2]),
    new Course(8, 'Machine Learning', [1, 2]),
    new Course(9, 'Distributed Systems', [5]),
    new Course(10, 'Cybersecurity', [2, 3]),
    new Course(11, 'Cloud Computing', [2, 3]),
    new Course(12, 'Mobile App Development', [4]),
    new Course(13, 'Game Development', [0]),
    new Course(14, 'Artificial Intelligence', [2, 8]),
    new Course(15, 'Big Data Analytics', [2, 3]),
    new Course(16, 'Blockchain Technology', [2, 3]),
    new Course(17, 'UI/UX Design', [14]),
    new Course(18, 'Embedded Systems', [1, 5]),
    new Course(19, 'Computer Graphics', [0])
];

const student = new Student(1, 'John Doe', [0, 1, 2, 3, 4]);

const targetCourses = [
  courses[13], //Game Development
  courses[16], //Blockchain Technology
  courses[17], //UI/UX Design (student cannot enroll)
  courses[18]  //Embedded Systems
];

console.log(`Enrollment status for ${student.name}:`);
for (const course of targetCourses) {
  if (course.canEnroll(student)) {
    console.log(`- Can enroll in ${course.name}`);
  } else {
    console.log(`- Cannot enroll in ${course.name} due to missing prerequisites.`);
  }
}
```

Listing 1-3: universityCourses.js

We create sample courses and a sample user that is still at the earlier stages of studies. We then try to find out if this student can enroll on 4 specific courses. We will see that the student will not be able to enroll at the most advanced ones, for lack of successfully completed prerequisite courses.

You can run this code with Node.js:

```
node universityCourses.js
```

You can find this project in GitHub:

https://github.com/htset/js_exercises_dsa/tree/master/UniversityCourses

2. Restaurant Reservations

For this exercise, we will create a small program that will create table reservations for a restaurant. Each table is characterized by its capacity. For simplicity, we will split the reservation time into one-hour slots; a reservation can span multiple consecutive slots.

Proposed Solution

First, we will define the class for a customer:

```
class Customer {
  constructor(name) {
    this.name = name;
  }
}
```

Listing 2-1: restaurant.js

This class contains the name of the customer. It could also include the customer phone number or other details.

Next, we define a class for the restaurant tables:

```
class Table {
  constructor(id, capacity) {
    this.id = id;
    this.capacity = capacity;
  }
}
```

Listing 2-2: restaurant.js

Each table object contains its ID as well as information about its capacity.

Next, we define the Reservation class:

```
class Reservation {
  constructor(customer, table, startTimeSlot, endTimeSlot) {
    this.customer = customer;
    this.table = table;
    this.startTimeSlot = startTimeSlot;
    this.endTimeSlot = endTimeSlot;
  }
}
```

Listing 2-3: restaurant.js

Each reservation contains references to Customer and Table objects. It also contains the starting and the ending time slot (not inclusive).

We also create a Restaurant class that will implement the functionality for the creation of new reservations:

```javascript
class Restaurant {
  constructor() {
    this.tables = [];
    this.reservations = [];
  }

  addTable(table) {
    this.tables.push(table);
  }

  isTableAvailable(table, startTimeSlot, endTimeSlot) {
    return !this.reservations.some(reservation =>
      reservation.table.id === table.id &&
      (
        (startTimeSlot >= reservation.startTimeSlot
          && startTimeSlot < reservation.endTimeSlot) ||
        (endTimeSlot > reservation.startTimeSlot
          && endTimeSlot <= reservation.endTimeSlot) ||
        (startTimeSlot <= reservation.startTimeSlot
          && endTimeSlot >= reservation.endTimeSlot)
      )
    );
  }

  findAvailableTables(capacity, startTimeSlot, endTimeSlot) {
    const availableTables = this.tables.filter(table =>
      table.capacity >= capacity
        && this.isTableAvailable(table, startTimeSlot, endTimeSlot)
    );
    availableTables.sort((a, b) => a.capacity - b.capacity);
    return availableTables;
  }

  addReservation(name, capacity, startSlot, endSlot) {
    const availableTables = this.findAvailableTables(capacity, startSlot, endSlot);
    if (availableTables.length > 0) {
      this.reservations.push(
        new Reservation(new Customer(name),
          availableTables[0],
          startSlot,
          endSlot)
      );
      console.log("Reservation successfully added.");
    } else {
      console.log("No available tables for the requested time slot.");
    }
  }

  printReservations() {
    console.log("All reservations:");
    for (const reservation of this.reservations) {
      console.log(`Customer: ${reservation.customer.name},
        Table Capacity: ${reservation.table.capacity},
        Start Time Slot: ${reservation.startTimeSlot},
```

```
        End Time Slot: ${reservation.endTimeSlot}`);
    }
  }
}
```
Listing 2-4: restaurant.js

Function `addTable()` adds the reference of a table into the `tables` array.

Function `isTableAvailable()` uses the array `some()` function to determine whether a table is reserved or not, in the specified timeslot.

Function `findAvailableTables()` filters the tables array in order to find all the tables that are available inside the specified timeslot. The tables that are found are then returned in a new array. The new array is then sorted in ascending order, according to the table capacity, as we are trying to fill the smallest tables first.

Next, the `addReservation()` function will create a new reservation on the fly and will insert it into the `reservations` array. That's of course, if a suitable table is found. Note that we get the first table in the sorted array, i.e. the table with the smallest capacity.

Finally, we use those classes to make new reservations:

```
const restaurant = new Restaurant();

//Add tables
restaurant.addTable(new Table(1, 6));
restaurant.addTable(new Table(2, 4));
restaurant.addTable(new Table(3, 2));

//Find available tables for a new reservation
restaurant.addReservation("Customer 1", 4, 1, 3);
restaurant.addReservation("Customer 2", 6, 2, 4);
restaurant.addReservation("Customer 3", 4, 3, 5);
restaurant.addReservation("Customer 4", 4, 1, 3);

restaurant.printReservations();
```
Listing 2-5: restaurant.js

We add tables to the `restaurant` object and try to make reservations for specific capacities and timeslots. Some will be successful, but for others there will not be any table available. At the end, we print all the available reservations in the system.

You can run this code with Node.js:

```
node restaurant.js
```

You can find this project in GitHub:

https://github.com/htset/js_exercises_dsa/tree/master/Restaurant

3. Library

Here we will create a console application for a library. Users will be able to enter books and list all the titles available in the library. They will also be able to lend books, return books as well as list all the book lending events. The books and the lending events will be stored in text files.

Proposed Solution

Let's begin with the definition of the `Book` and `LendingEvent` classes:

```
const fs = require('fs');
const readline = require('readline');

class Book {
  constructor(title, author, available) {
    this.Title = title;
    this.Author = author;
    this.Available = available;
  }
}

class LendingEvent {
  constructor(bookTitle, userName, lendingDate, returned) {
    this.BookTitle = bookTitle;
    this.UserName = userName;
    this.LendingDate = lendingDate;
    this.Returned = returned;
  }
}
```

Listing 3-1: library.js

For each book, we record the title and the author. We also keep information about whether it is available or is currently lent.

For each lending event we record the book title and the name of the library user that has borrowed it. We also keep the lending date as well as an integer value of whether it has been returned or not (1 or 0 respectively).

We also define the `Library` class, that contains all the functionality for adding and displaying book information:

```
class Library {
  constructor() {
    this.BooksFilename = 'books.txt';
    this.LendingFilename = 'lending_events.txt';
    this.rl = readline.createInterface({
      input: process.stdin,
      output: process.stdout
    });
  }
```

Listing 3-2: library.js

`readline` is a built-in Node.js module that provides an interface for reading data from a readable stream (like `process.stdin`), line by line. It is particularly useful for creating command-line interfaces (CLIs) where user input needs to be captured interactively.

Class `Library`'s first function is used to add a new book in library catalog:

```javascript
async addBook() {
  const book = new Book();

  book.Title = await this.question('Book title: ');
  book.Author = await this.question('Author: ');
  book.Available = 1;

  fs.appendFileSync(this.BooksFilename,
    `${book.Title}|${book.Author}|${book.Available}\n`);

  console.log('Book added successfully.');
}
```

Listing 3-3: library.js

At the beginning, we ask the user for the book title and author. Then we append the new book information into the books text file. The following format is used:

```
book title|book author|Available (0 or 1)
```

The `question()` function is defined outside of the class:

```javascript
async question(prompt) {
  return new Promise((resolve) => {
    this.rl.question(prompt, (answer) => {
      resolve(answer);
    });
  });
}
```

Listing 3-4: library.js

Next, we implement the listing of the books:

```javascript
listBooks() {
  if (!fs.existsSync(this.BooksFilename)) {
    console.log('No books entered so far');
    return;
  }

  console.log('Books available in the library:');
  const lines = fs.readFileSync(this.BooksFilename, 'utf8').split('\n');
  lines.forEach(line => {
    if (line.trim() !== '') {
```

```
      const parts = line.split('|');
      console.log(`Title: ${parts[0]}`);
      console.log(`Author: ${parts[1]}`);
      console.log(`Available: ${parts[2] === '1' ? 'True' : 'False'}`);
      console.log('-------------------------------');
    }
  });
}
```

Listing 3-5: library.js

Here, we read the contents of the file into a string. We split the string into multiple lines, and then we split each line into tokens based on the separator (|).

We proceed with the book lending functionality:

```
async lendBook() {
  if (!fs.existsSync(this.BooksFilename)) {
    console.log('No books entered so far');
    return;
  }

  let bookTitle = await this.question('Enter the title of the book to lend: ');

  let lines = fs.readFileSync(this.BooksFilename, 'utf8').split('\n');
  let bookFound = false;

  for (let i = 0; i < lines.length; i++) {
    const parts = lines[i].split('|');
    if (parts[0] === bookTitle && parts[2] === '1') {
      lines[i] = `${parts[0]}|${parts[1]}|0`;
      bookFound = true;

      let userName = await this.question('Enter your name: ');

      fs.appendFileSync(this.LendingFilename,
        `${bookTitle}|${userName}|${new Date()}|0\n`);
      console.log(`Book '${bookTitle}' has been lent to ${userName}.`);

      break;
    }
  }

  if (!bookFound) {
    console.log(`Book '${bookTitle}' not found or not available.`);
  }

  fs.writeFileSync(this.BooksFilename, lines.join('\n'));
}
```

Listing 3-6: library.js

We first try to find the requested book by reading all the entries in the books file. The entries will be stored in an array of strings.

We iterate this array and we split each entry into the book details (title, author, availability). When we find the book (and if it is available), we mark it as not available.

Afterwards, we record the lending event by writing a new entry at the end of the respective file. Finally, we write all the entries in the array back to the books text file, overwriting the file.

Next, we present the functionality for returning a book:

```
async returnBook() {
  if (!fs.existsSync(this.LendingFilename)) {
    console.log('No lending events entered so far');
    return;
  }

  let bookTitle = await this.question('Enter the title of the book to return: ');

  let booksLines = fs.readFileSync(this.BooksFilename, 'utf8').split('\n');
  let bookFound = false;

  for (let i = 0; i < booksLines.length; i++) {
    const parts = booksLines[i].split('|');
    if (parts[0] === bookTitle && parts[2] === '0') {
      booksLines[i] = `${parts[0]}|${parts[1]}|1`;
      bookFound = true;

      let lendingLines = fs.readFileSync(this.LendingFilename, 'utf8').split('\n');

      for (let j = 0; j < lendingLines.length; j++) {
        const lendingParts = lendingLines[j].split('|');
        if (lendingParts[0] === bookTitle && lendingParts[3] === '0') {
          lendingLines[j] =
            `${lendingParts[0]}|${lendingParts[1]}|${lendingParts[2]}|1`;
          console.log(`Book '${bookTitle}' has been returned.`);
          break;
        }
      }

      fs.writeFileSync(this.LendingFilename, lendingLines.join('\n'));
      break;
    }
  }

  if (!bookFound) {
    console.log(`Book '${bookTitle}' not found or already returned.`);
  }

  fs.writeFileSync(this.BooksFilename, booksLines.join('\n'));
}
```

Listing 3-7: library.js

Here, we read again all the book file entries into an array of strings, and we try to find the requested file. Then, we read all the book lending events from the respective file and we search for the lending event of the specific book.

If we find the event, then we change its status to "returned" and we write all the entries back to the lending file. Finally, we also store all the book entries into the respective file, after having changed the book availability status back to 1 again.

Now, let's see the events listing function:

```
listLendingEvents() {
  if (!fs.existsSync(this.LendingFilename)) {
    console.log('No lending events entered so far');
    return;
  }

  console.log('Lending events:');
  const lines = fs.readFileSync(this.LendingFilename, 'utf8').split('\n');
  lines.forEach(line => {
    if (line.trim() !== '') {
      const parts = line.split('|');
      console.log(`Book Title: ${parts[0]}`);
      console.log(`User Name: ${parts[1]}`);
      console.log(`Lending Date: ${parts[2]}`);
      console.log(`Returned: ${parts[3] === '1' ? 'True' : 'False'}`);
      console.log('-------------------------------');
    }
  });
}
```

Listing 3-8: library.js

And finally, the `menu()` function that handles the interaction with the user:

```
async menu() {
  let choice;

  do {
    console.log('\n1. Add a book\n2. List all books\n' +
      '3. Lend a book\n4. Return a book\n5. List lending events\n0. Exit');
    choice = parseInt(await this.question('Enter your choice: '));

    switch (choice) {
      case 1:
        await this.addBook();
        break;
      case 2:
        this.listBooks();
        break;
      case 3:
        await this.lendBook();
        break;
      case 4:
```

```
          await this.returnBook();
          break;
        case 5:
          this.listLendingEvents();
          break;
        case 0:
          console.log('Exiting.');
          break;
        default:
          console.log('Invalid choice. Please try again.');
          break;
      }

    } while (choice !== 0);

    this.rl.close(); //Close readline interface after all operations are done
  }
}

//Run the main function
(async () => {
  const lib = new Library();
  await lib.menu();
})();
```

Listing 3-9: library.js

You can run this code with Node.js:

`node library.js`

You can find this project in GitHub:

https://github.com/htset/js_exercises_dsa/tree/master/Library

4. Contact List

In this exercise, we will create a list that will store the names and the phone numbers of our contacts. For faster search performance, the contacts will be stored in a *hash map* structure.

Proposed Solution

A *hash map*, also known as a *hash table*, is a data structure that efficiently organizes and retrieves data based on key-value pairs. It employs a technique called *hashing*, where each key is mapped to a unique index in an array using a hash function. This mapping allows for rapid insertion, deletion, and retrieval of values based on their associated keys.

In cases where multiple keys hash to the same index (known as *collisions*), hash maps often employ strategies such as *chaining* to handle these collisions gracefully and maintain performance.

Here is the definition of the classes used:

```
class Contact {
  constructor() {
    this.name = null;
    this.phone = null;
    this.next = null;
  }
}

class ContactList {
  constructor() {
    this.HASH_SIZE = 100;
    this.bucketTable = new Array(this.HASH_SIZE).fill(null);
  }

  ...
```

Listing 4-1: contactList.js

The `ContactList` class contains a table of 100 entries. Each entry contains a reference to a `Contact` object. The `Contact` class contains the name and the phone number, as well as a reference to another `Contact` object, making it a linked list node. Essentially, the `ContactList` class is an array of linked lists; in this way the contact list can expand as we add new elements, avoiding collisions.

A contact will be inserted into one of the buckets according to its specific hash number. We will use a hash function that will create a number between 0 and 99 based on the contact's name string:

```
  hash(name) {
    let hash = 0;
    for (let i = 0; i < name.length; i++) {
      const charCode = name.charCodeAt(i);
      hash = ((hash << 5) + hash) + charCode;
```

```
  }
  return hash % this.HASH_SIZE;
}
```
Listing 4-2: contactList.js

This function is based on a hash function written by Daniel J. Bernstein (also know as *djb*)[1]. This function returns the index of the hash map, where we should insert the specific contact.

In the class constructor we initialize the buckets with nulls:

```
constructor() {
  this.HASH_SIZE = 100;
  this.bucketTable = new Array(this.HASH_SIZE).fill(null);
}
```
Listing 4-3: contactList.js

Here is the code for the contact addition:

```
contactAdd(name, phone) {
  const hashIndex = this.hash(name);
  const newContact = new Contact();
  newContact.name = name;
  newContact.phone = phone;
  newContact.next = this.bucketTable[hashIndex];
  this.bucketTable[hashIndex] = newContact;
}
```
Listing 4-4: contactList.js

We first calculate the hash index based on the contact's name and then we create a new Contact object. After populating the object properties, we insert the object at the beginning of the respective bucket.

Here is the code for contact removal:

```
contactRemove(name) {
  const index = this.hash(name);
  let contact = this.bucketTable[index];
  let previous = null;

  while (contact !== null) {
    if (contact.name === name) {
      if (previous === null) {
        //Contact to remove is the head of the list
        this.bucketTable[index] = contact.next;
      } else {
        //Contact to remove is not the head of the list
        previous.next = contact.next;
      }
```

---

[1] http://www.cse.yorku.ca/~oz/hash.html

```
      console.log(`Contact '${name}' removed successfully.`);
      return;
    }
    previous = contact;
    contact = contact.next;
  }
  console.log(`Contact '${name}' not found.`);
}
```

Listing 4-5: contactList.js

To remove an entry, we first need to get its hash value. We use this integer value as the index to get the respective bucket. We then search the bucket entries, one by one, until we locate the specific contact. We then remove the entry from the buckets, in the same way we remove a node from a linked list.

Next, the code for contact search is presented:

```
contactSearch(name) {
  const hashIndex = this.hash(name);
  let contact = this.bucketTable[hashIndex];
  while (contact !== null) {
    if (contact.name === name) {
      console.log(`Name: ${contact.name}\nPhone Number: ${contact.phone}`);
      return;
    }
    contact = contact.next;
  }
  console.log(`Contact '${name}' not found.`);
}
}
```

Listing 4-6: contactList.js

Finally, we create a phonebook and we use it to add, remove and search contacts:

```
const phonebook = new ContactList();
phonebook.contactAdd("John", "235454545");
phonebook.contactAdd("Jane", "775755454");
phonebook.contactAdd("George", "4344343477");

phonebook.contactSearch("John");
phonebook.contactSearch("Alex");
phonebook.contactSearch("George");

phonebook.contactRemove("Jake");
phonebook.contactRemove("Jane");
phonebook.contactSearch("Jane");
```

Listing 4-7: contactList.js

You can run this code with Node.js:

```
node contactList.js
```

You can find this project in GitHub:

https://github.com/htset/js_exercises_dsa/tree/master/ContactList

5. Priority Todo List

We are going to implement a simple todo list application. Each entry will contain the task description as well as a number that will signify its priority (top priority is equal to 1).

The todo list will be implemented using a *linked list*. Apart from the options to add, delete and display tasks, there will also be functionality to sort the linked list using *bubble sort*.

Proposed Solution

This exercise will be implemented with a web page. Here is the HTML file:

```html
<!DOCTYPE html>
<html lang="en">
<head>
  <meta charset="UTF-8">
  <title>Todo List</title>
  <style>
    body {
      font-family: Arial, sans-serif;
      padding: 20px;
    }
    .todo-form, .remove-form {
      display: flex;
      gap: 10px;
      margin-bottom: 20px;
    }
    .todo-list {
      list-style-type: none;
      padding: 0;
    }
    .todo-item {
      margin-bottom: 5px;
      padding: 10px;
      background-color: #f0f0f0;
      border-radius: 5px;
    }
  </style>
</head>
<body>
  <h1>Todo List Manager</h1>

  <form id="todoForm" class="todo-form">
    <input type="text" id="description"
      placeholder="Enter task description">
    <input type="number" id="priority"
      placeholder="Enter priority">
    <button type="submit">Add Task</button>
  </form>

  <form id="removeForm" class="remove-form">
    <input type="number" id="removeIndex"
      placeholder="Enter task number to remove">
    <button type="submit">Remove Task</button>
```

```html
  </form>

  <button id="sortButton">Sort Tasks by Priority</button>

  <ul id="todoList" class="todo-list">
    <!-- Todo items will be added dynamically here -->
  </ul>

  <script src="todo.js"></script>
</body>
</html>
```

Listing 5-1: index.html

The web page contains the following functionality:

- an input form to insert new Todos
- an input form to enter the Todo number for deletion
- a button to sort the existing Todos
- a list that will contain the Todos

Here is the definition of the linked list structure at the start of the source file (Todo.js):

```
class Task {
  constructor(description, priority) {
    this.description = description;
    this.priority = priority;
    this.next = null;
  }
}

class TodoList {
  constructor() {
    this.head = null;
    this.size = 0;
  }

  ...
```

Listing 5-2: todo.js

The linked list consists of Task nodes that get linked one to the other via the next reference. The head variable points to the first element in the list.

The addTask() function creates a new task node and inserts it at the end of the linked list:

```
  addTask(description, priority) {
    const task = new Task(description, priority);
    task.next = null;

    if (this.head === null) {
      //List is empty
      this.head = task;
```

```
    }
    else {
      let temp = this.head;
      //Find the last node
      while (temp.next !== null) {
        temp = temp.next;
      }
      //Insert the new task after the last node
      temp.next = task;
    }
    this.size++;
    return task;
  }
```

Listing 5-3: todo.js

Next, we define the `removeTask()` function:

```
  removeTask(index) {
    if (index < 0 || index >= this.size) {
      console.error("Index out of bounds.");
      return;
    }

    if (index === 0) {
      //Removing the first item
      this.head = this.head.next;
    }
    else {
      let current = this.head;
      let previous = null;
      let i = 0;

      while (i < index) {
        previous = current;
        current = current.next;
        i++;
      }

      if (previous !== null) {
        previous.next = current.next;
      }
    }

    this.size--;
  }
```

Listing 5-4: todo.js

The argument to the function is the index of the entry inside the linked list, as it is presented during task listing in the web page. As we will see in the next snippet, we start listing the tasks from number 1, which is something that we take into account in the calculations above.

Here is the code for the task listing:

```javascript
displayTasks() {
  let temp = this.head;
  const todoListElem = document.getElementById("todoList");
  todoListElem.innerHTML = ""; //Clear previous list

  let index = 1;
  while (temp !== null) {
    const li = document.createElement("li");
    li.className = "todo-item";
    li.textContent = `${index}) Description: ${temp.description},
                    Priority: ${temp.priority}`;
    todoListElem.appendChild(li);
    temp = temp.next;
    index++;
  }
}
```

Listing 5-5: todo.js

We empty the existing list and then we create new `<li>` elements that will contain the Todo entries.

Finally, we present the code for the sorting of tasks according to their priority:

```javascript
sortTasks() {
  //Bubble sort (descending order)
  let swapped;
  let ptr1;
  let ptr2 = null;

  if (this.head === null)
    return;

  do {
    swapped = false; //will change if swapping happens
    ptr1 = this.head;

    while (ptr1.next !== ptr2) {
      if (ptr1.priority > ptr1.next.priority) {
        //Swap data of adjacent nodes
        let tempPriority = ptr1.priority;
        ptr1.priority = ptr1.next.priority;
        ptr1.next.priority = tempPriority;

        let tempDescription = ptr1.description;
        ptr1.description = ptr1.next.description;
        ptr1.next.description = tempDescription;

        swapped = true; //swap happened in this loop pass; don't stop yet
      }
      ptr1 = ptr1.next;
    }
```

```
      ptr2 = ptr1;
    } while (swapped == true); //quit loop when no swap happened
  }
}
```
Listing 5-6: todo.js

The code employs the *bubble sort* algorithm to perform the task sorting operation. In bubble sort, we perform multiple passes of the linked list. Each time we find a task that has lower priority than its next task, then we perform swapping of those adjacent tasks. Over time, all entries will be sorted according to priority and there will eventually be a loop pass where no swapping will occur. This is when the algorithm will end.

Finally, here is the initialization code, where event listeners are assigned to the three forms in the HTML page:

```
const todoList = new TodoList();

const todoForm = document.getElementById("todoForm");

//add submit event listener to Add Task form
todoForm.addEventListener("submit", function(event) {
  event.preventDefault();

  const description = document.getElementById("description").value;
  const priority = parseInt(document.getElementById("priority").value);

  if (isNaN(priority)) {
    alert("Priority must be a number.");
    return;
  }

  todoList.addTask(description, priority);
  todoList.displayTasks();

  //Clear input fields
  document.getElementById("description").value = "";
  document.getElementById("priority").value = "";
});

const removeForm = document.getElementById("removeForm");

//add submit event listener to Remove Task form
removeForm.addEventListener("submit", function(event) {
  event.preventDefault();

  const index = parseInt(document.getElementById("removeIndex").value);

  if (isNaN(index)) {
    alert("Index must be a number.");
    return;
  }
```

```
  if (index < 1 || index > todoList.size) {
    alert("Index out of bounds.");
    return;
  }

  todoList.removeTask(index - 1);
  todoList.displayTasks();

  //Clear input field
  document.getElementById("removeIndex").value = "";
});

const sortButton = document.getElementById("sortButton");

//add submit event listener to Sort Tasks form
sortButton.addEventListener("click", function(event) {
  todoList.sortTasks();
  todoList.displayTasks();
});
```

Listing 5-7: todo.js

To run this exercise, you can open *index.html* in a browser window.

You can find this project in GitHub:

https://github.com/htset/js_exercises_dsa/tree/master/Todo

6. Songs List

Let's create a simple program that takes an array of songs and sorts them by artist, album or release date, using *insertion sort*.

Proposed Solution

The Song class will contain information about the title of the song, the artist, the album and the release year:

```
class Song {
  constructor(title, artist, album, releaseYear) {
    this.title = title;
    this.artist = artist;
    this.album = album;
    this.releaseYear = releaseYear;
  }
}
```

Listing 6-1: songs.js

Next, we define three functions, that will be used for the comparisons:

```
class Songs {
  //Compare songs based on artist
  static compareByArtist(a, b) {
    return a.artist === b.artist;
  }

  //Compare songs based on album
  static compareByAlbum(a, b) {
    return a.album === b.album;
  }

  //Compare songs based on release date
  static compareByReleaseDate(a, b) {
    return a.releaseYear - b.releaseYear;
  }

  ...
```

Listing 6-2: songs.js

In the first two functions, we compare two strings, while in the third one we compare two integers. Those functions will be used by the `insertionSort()` function:

```
static insertionSort(arr, compare) {
  const n = arr.length;
  for (let i = 1; i < n; i++) {
    const key = arr[i];
    let j = i - 1;

    //Move elements of arr[0..i-1], that are greater than key,
    //to one position ahead of their current position
```

```
        while (j >= 0 && compare(arr[j], key) > 0) {
            arr[j + 1] = arr[j];
            j = j - 1;
        }
        arr[j + 1] = key;
    }
}

...
```
Listing 6-3: songs.js

The `compare` argument is a function used as a parameter for the `insertionSort()` function to specify the comparison logic for sorting the songs array.

For instance, if we call `insertionSort()` like this:

```
Songs.insertionSort(songs, Songs.compareByArtist);
```

then, the following code inside `insertionSort()`:

```
while (j >= 0 && compare(arr[j], key) > 0)
```

will result in calling the `compareByArtist()` function. In this way, we don't have to write `insertionSort()` three times to accommodate for the three different types of comparison.

Insertion sort works by taking each element in the array and moving it to the left part of the array in a sorted position. At any time, the left part of the array is sorted, while we take items from the right part. As we move an element to a place in the array, all the items to the right will have to move one place to the right.

This is all illustrated in the `main()` function where we call `insertionSort()` three times, each time passing a different comparison function. Each time, the array is sorted in a different way:

```
static main() {
    const songs = [
        new Song('Song1', 'Artist2', 'Album1', 2010),
        new Song('Song2', 'Artist1', 'Album2', 2005),
        new Song('Song3', 'Artist3', 'Album1', 2015),
        new Song('Song4', 'Artist4', 'Album3', 2008),
        new Song('Song5', 'Artist1', 'Album2', 2003),
        new Song('Song6', 'Artist3', 'Album4', 2019),
        new Song('Song7', 'Artist2', 'Album3', 2012),
        new Song('Song8', 'Artist4', 'Album4', 2017),
        new Song('Song9', 'Artist5', 'Album5', 2014),
        new Song('Song10', 'Artist5', 'Album5', 2011),
    ];

    const numSongs = songs.length;
```

```
    //Sort by artist
    Songs.insertionSort(songs, Songs.compareByArtist);
    console.log('Sorted by Artist:');
    songs.forEach(song => {
      console.log(`${song.title} from ${song.artist}`);
    });
    console.log();

    //Sort by album
    Songs.insertionSort(songs, Songs.compareByAlbum);
    console.log('Sorted by Album:');
    songs.forEach(song => {
      console.log(`${song.title} from ${song.album}`);
    });
    console.log();

    //Sort by release date
    Songs.insertionSort(songs, Songs.compareByReleaseDate);
    console.log('Sorted by Release Date:');
    songs.forEach(song => {
      console.log(`${song.title} released in ${song.releaseYear}`);
    });
  }
}

Songs.main();
```

Listing 6-4: songs.js

You can run this code with Node.js:

`node songs.js`

You can find this project in GitHub:

https://github.com/htset/js_exercises_dsa/tree/master/Songs

7. Task allocation

We will create a program where users can enter the description of tasks and their durations. The tasks will be allocated to workers, based on the amount of work that they already have taken over. This means that the task will be allocated to the worker with the lower workload.

Proposed Solution

This exercise will be implemented with a web page. Here is the HTML file:

```html
<!DOCTYPE html>
<html lang="en">

<head>
  <meta charset="UTF-8">
  <title>Task Allocation</title>
  <style>
    body {
      font-family: Arial, sans-serif;
      margin: 20px;
    }

    form {
      margin-bottom: 20px;
    }

    input[type="text"],
    input[type="number"] {
      margin-bottom: 10px;
      display: block;
    }

    .tasks,
    .workers {
      margin-top: 20px;
    }
  </style>
</head>

<body>
  <h1>Task Allocation</h1>
  <form id="taskForm">
    <label for="description">Task Description:</label>
    <input type="text" id="description" required>
    <label for="duration">Task Duration (in minutes):</label>
    <input type="number" id="duration" required>
    <button type="submit">Add Task</button>
  </form>

  <div class="tasks">
    <h2>Tasks</h2>
    <ul id="taskList"></ul>
```

```html
    </div>

    <div class="workers">
      <h2>Workers Queue</h2>
      <ul id="workerList"></ul>
    </div>

    <script src="taskAllocation.js"></script>
</body>

</html>
```

Listing 7-1: index.html

We will use a priority queue to express the differences in priority between the various workers, based on their workload so far.

Let's first define the Task and Worker classes:

```js
class Task {
  constructor(description, duration) {
    this.description = description;
    this.duration = duration;
  }
}

class Worker {
  constructor(id, workload) {
    this.id = id;
    this.workload = workload;
  }
}
```

Listing 7-2: taskAllocation.js

The Task class consists of the task description and duration in minutes. The Worker class contains the ID of the worker as well as the workload (also in minutes).

Next, we define PriorityQueue class:

```js
class PriorityQueue {
  constructor() {
    this.workers = [];
  }

  enqueue(worker) {
    let added = false;

    for (let i = 0; i < this.workers.length; i++) {
      if (this.workers[i].workload > worker.workload) {
        this.workers.splice(i, 0, worker);
        added = true;
        break;
      }
```

```
    }
    if (!added) {
      this.workers.push(worker);
    }
  }
  
  dequeue() {
    return this.workers.shift();
  }
  
  get count() {
    return this.workers.length;
  }
}
```
Listing 7-3: taskAllocation.js

When we enqueue a new worker object into the PriorityQueue class, the worker is inserted according to the priority i.e., the workload that has already been undertaken by this worker. Moreover, when we dequeue an item from the queue, we get the first item, i.e. the item with the highest priority (→ lowest workload).

Next, we define the TaskAllocation class, that contains three static functions:

```
class TaskAllocation {
  static addTask(workerQueue, tasks) {
    const description = document.getElementById('description').value;
    const duration = parseInt(document.getElementById('duration').value, 10);
    
    if (workerQueue.count === 0) {
      alert("No workers available! Task cannot be assigned.");
      return;
    }
    
    //Dequeue the worker with the shortest workload
    const worker = workerQueue.dequeue();
    
    //Assign the task to the worker and update workload
    tasks.push(new Task(description, duration));
    alert(`Task added successfully and allocated to Worker ${worker.id}!`);
    
    //Update workload
    worker.workload += duration;
    workerQueue.enqueue(worker);
  }
  
  static displayTasks(tasks, taskList) {
    taskList.innerHTML = '';
    tasks.forEach(task => {
      const li = document.createElement('li');
      li.textContent = `Task description: ${task.description},
        Duration: ${task.duration} minutes`;
      taskList.appendChild(li);
```

```
    });
  }

  static displayWorkers(workerQueue, workerList) {
    workerList.innerHTML = '';
    workerQueue.workers.forEach(item => {
      const li = document.createElement('li');
      li.textContent = `Worker ID: ${item.id},
        Workload: ${item.workload} minutes`;
      workerList.appendChild(li);
    });
  }
}
```
Listing 7-4: taskAllocation.js

Those functions are used to add a new task to a worker, to display the tasks list and to display the workers list.

To find the worker that has the lowest workload, we store workers in the priority queue. Note that we are using the `workload` property as the parameter that will be used to sort the priority queue. When we dequeue an item from the queue, then we will get the item with the lowest workload.

In `addTask()`, we get the worker with the lowest workload (the one that is positioned at the front of the queue) and we add the task's workload to the worker's own workload. Then, we store the task into the tasks list. Finally, the worker is inserted into the queue again; now the worker will be positioned according to the newly updated workload.

The above functions are used by the following event handler:

```
document.addEventListener('DOMContentLoaded', () => {
  const tasks = [];
  const workerQueue = new PriorityQueue();
  const numWorkers = parseInt(prompt("Enter the number of workers: "), 10);

  //Initialize workers with ID and 0 workload
  for (let i = 0; i < numWorkers; i++) {
    workerQueue.enqueue(new Worker(i, 0));
  }

  const taskForm = document.getElementById('taskForm');
  const taskList = document.getElementById('taskList');
  const workerList = document.getElementById('workerList');

  taskForm.addEventListener('submit', (e) => {
    e.preventDefault();
    TaskAllocation.addTask(workerQueue, tasks);
    TaskAllocation.displayTasks(tasks, taskList);
    TaskAllocation.displayWorkers(workerQueue, workerList);
  });
```

```
});
```
Listing 7-5: taskAllocation.js

The event listener fires when the DOM content has been loaded. First, it asks the user about the number of workers that will be used and creates a priority queue accordingly.

To run this exercise, you should open *index.html* in a browser window.

You can find this project in GitHub:

https://github.com/htset/js_exercises_dsa/tree/master/TaskAllocation

8. Word Frequencies

We will create a simple program that will parse a text file and will find the frequencies of all the words that appear in it.

Proposed Solution

This project is a use case for a dictionary structure. We will use a plain JavaScript object that will store word and word frequency pairs.

Here is the program code:

```
const fs = require('fs');

//Clean a word by removing non-letter characters and converting to lowercase
function cleanWord(word) {
  return word.replace(/[^a-zA-Z]/g, '').toLowerCase();
}

const wordFrequency = {};

//Read text from file
const data = fs.readFileSync('input.txt', 'utf8');
const lines = data.split('\n');

for (const line of lines) {
  const words = line.split(' ').filter(word => word !== '');

  for (const word of words) {
    const cleanedWord = cleanWord(word);
    if (cleanedWord) {
      if (wordFrequency[cleanedWord]) {
        wordFrequency[cleanedWord]++;
      } else {
        wordFrequency[cleanedWord] = 1;
      }
    }
  }
}

//Display word frequencies
console.log('Word Frequencies:');
for (const [word, frequency] of Object.entries(wordFrequency)) {
  console.log(`${word}: ${frequency}`);
}
```

Listing 8-1: wordFrequencies.js

First, we are reading the input file, line by line. Then, we split each line, based on spaces and we process each word to make it lowercase and remove non-letter characters.

Then, we check if the dictionary already contains this word. If that's the case, then we increment the respective integer value by one. Otherwise, we create a new entry in the dictionary.

Finally, we employ a loop to print all the words and their frequencies to the console.

You can run this code with Node.js:

```
node wordFrequencies.js
```

You can find this project in GitHub:

https://github.com/htset/js_exercises_dsa/tree/master/WordFrequencies

9. Syntax Checker

Let's create a trivial syntax checker that will scan a source code file and will determine whether the parentheses, brackets, or braces in the code are balanced or not.

Proposed Solution

In source code, when we open a series of parentheses, brackets, or braces, we have to make sure that they are closed in the reverse order.

The fact that items entered in a *stack* are extracted in the reverse order, makes it suitable for this algorithm:

```
const fs = require('fs');
const readline = require('readline');

//Stack class
class Stack {
  constructor() {
    this.items = [];
  }

  //Push a character onto the stack
  push(c) {
    this.items.push(c);
  }

  //Pop a character from the stack
  pop() {
    if (this.items.length === 0) {
      console.log('Stack is empty');
      process.exit(1);
    }
    return this.items.pop();
  }

  //Check if the stack is empty
  checkEmpty() {
    return this.items.length === 0;
  }
}
```

Listing 9-1: syntaxChecker.js

The most interesting part of the code is the algorithm that checks whether the file is balanced or not:

```
//Function to check if the syntax in a file is balanced
function checkBalanced(filename) {
  const stack = new Stack();
  const data = fs.readFileSync(filename, 'utf8');

  for (let i = 0; i < data.length; i++) {
```

```
    const c = data[i];

    if (c === '(' || c === '[' || c === '{') {
      stack.push(c);
    } else if (c === ')' || c === ']' || c === '}') {
      if (stack.checkEmpty()) {
        return 0;
      }

      const openingChar = stack.pop();

      if (
        (c === ')' && openingChar !== '(') ||
        (c === ']' && openingChar !== '[') ||
        (c === '}' && openingChar !== '{')
      ) {
        return 0;
      }
    }
  }

  return stack.checkEmpty() ? 1 : 0;
}

//Main function to prompt for file path and check balance
function main() {
  const rl = readline.createInterface({
    input: process.stdin,
    output: process.stdout,
  });

  rl.question('Path to the source file: ', (filename) => {
    if (checkBalanced(filename) === 1) {
      console.log('The input file is balanced.');
    } else {
      console.log('The input file is not balanced.');
    }
    rl.close();
  });
}

main();
```

Listing 9-2: syntaxChecker.js

We open and parse the source code file, and we push the bracket *opening* characters into the stack. When we encounter a *closing* character, then we pop the first available opening character from the stack.

If there is a mismatch between those two characters, we conclude that the file is not balanced. At the end, we also check that the stack is emptied; if not, then the file is still unbalanced.

Note that this is a trivial version of the algorithm. In fact, if we try to check the exercises's own source file (*syntaxChecker.js*) for parentheses balancing, we will get an error – even though the code compiles. That's because we use single characters (opening or closing) in our code during checking, like in the following line:

```
if (c == '(' || c == '[' || c == '{')
```

A more advanced version of the algorithm would not take those characters (e.g. those enclosed in quotes) into account.

You can run this code with Node.js:

```
node syntaxChecker.js
```

You can find this project in GitHub:

https://github.com/htset/js_exercises_dsa/tree/master/SyntaxChecker

10. Maze Solver

In this exercise, we will use a *stack* to find our way through a maze.

Proposed Solution

We will define a maze as a two-dimensional array of integers. The walls will be marked with ones (1), while the corridors of the maze will be marked with zeroes (0).

Below, we can see the definition of a 15x15 maze:

```
this.matrix = [
  [0, 1, 0, 0, 0, 0, 0, 0, 0, 0, 0, 0, 0, 0, 0],
  [0, 1, 0, 1, 0, 1, 1, 1, 1, 0, 1, 1, 1, 1, 0],
  [0, 1, 0, 1, 0, 1, 0, 0, 0, 0, 1, 0, 0, 0, 0],
  [0, 0, 0, 1, 0, 1, 0, 1, 1, 1, 1, 0, 1, 1, 0],
  [0, 1, 0, 1, 0, 1, 0, 0, 0, 0, 1, 0, 1, 0, 0],
  [0, 1, 0, 1, 0, 1, 1, 1, 1, 0, 1, 0, 1, 1, 0],
  [0, 1, 0, 1, 0, 0, 0, 0, 1, 0, 1, 0, 0, 0, 0],
  [0, 1, 0, 1, 1, 1, 1, 0, 1, 0, 1, 0, 1, 1, 0],
  [0, 1, 0, 0, 0, 0, 1, 0, 1, 0, 1, 0, 0, 1, 0],
  [0, 1, 1, 1, 1, 0, 1, 0, 1, 0, 1, 0, 1, 1, 0],
  [0, 0, 0, 0, 1, 0, 1, 0, 1, 0, 1, 0, 0, 0, 0],
  [0, 1, 1, 0, 1, 0, 1, 0, 1, 0, 1, 1, 1, 1, 0],
  [0, 0, 1, 0, 1, 0, 0, 0, 1, 0, 0, 0, 0, 1, 0],
  [0, 1, 1, 1, 1, 1, 1, 1, 1, 1, 1, 0, 1, 0],
  [0, 0, 0, 0, 0, 0, 0, 0, 0, 0, 0, 0, 0, 1, 0],
];
```

Listing 10-1: mazeSolver.js

The entrance of the maze is at the top left corner, and the exit at the bottom right corner.

We will use a stack structure to solve this maze. As we move through the maze, we store the entered point coordinates in the stack. When we reach a dead end, then we will have to backtrack, and we will do this by popping one point from the stack. This algorithm is called *Depth-first search (DFS)*, as it goes inside the maze as deep as possible, only to go back and try another direction when no way is found.

Here is the code for the coordinate points:

```
class Point {
  constructor(row = 0, col = 0) {
    this.row = row;
    this.col = col;
  }
}
```

Listing 10-2: mazeSolver.js

And here is the code for the stack:

```
class Stack {
```

```
constructor() {
  this.items = [];
}

//Push a character onto the stack
push(c) {
  this.items.push(c);
}

//Pop a character from the stack
pop() {
  if (this.items.length === 0) {
    console.log('Stack is empty');
    process.exit(1);
  }
  return this.items.pop();
}

//Check if the stack is empty
checkEmpty() {
  return this.items.length === 0;
}
}
```

Listing 10-3: mazeSolver.js

Now, it is time to introduce a class that will handle the maze:

```
class Maze {
  constructor() {
    this.ROWS = 15;
    this.COLS = 15;
    this.matrix = [
      [0, 1, 0, 0, 0, 0, 0, 0, 0, 0, 0, 0, 0, 0, 0],
      [0, 1, 0, 1, 0, 1, 1, 1, 1, 0, 1, 1, 1, 1, 0],
      [0, 1, 0, 1, 0, 1, 0, 0, 0, 0, 1, 0, 0, 0, 0],
      [0, 0, 0, 1, 0, 1, 0, 1, 1, 1, 1, 0, 1, 1, 0],
      [0, 1, 0, 1, 0, 1, 0, 0, 0, 0, 1, 0, 1, 0, 0],
      [0, 1, 0, 1, 0, 1, 1, 1, 1, 0, 1, 0, 1, 1, 0],
      [0, 1, 0, 1, 0, 0, 0, 0, 1, 0, 1, 0, 0, 0, 0],
      [0, 1, 0, 1, 1, 1, 1, 0, 1, 0, 1, 0, 1, 1, 0],
      [0, 1, 0, 0, 0, 0, 1, 0, 1, 0, 1, 0, 0, 1, 0],
      [0, 1, 1, 1, 1, 0, 1, 0, 1, 0, 1, 0, 1, 1, 0],
      [0, 0, 0, 0, 1, 0, 1, 0, 1, 0, 1, 0, 0, 0, 0],
      [0, 1, 1, 0, 1, 0, 1, 0, 1, 0, 1, 1, 1, 1, 0],
      [0, 0, 1, 0, 1, 0, 0, 0, 1, 0, 0, 0, 0, 1, 0],
      [0, 1, 1, 1, 1, 1, 1, 1, 1, 1, 1, 1, 0, 1, 0],
      [0, 0, 0, 0, 0, 0, 0, 0, 0, 0, 0, 0, 0, 1, 0],
    ];
    this.stack = new Stack();
  }

  ...
```

Listing 10-4: mazeSolver.js

Next, we add the code to check whether we can move to a cell:

```
canMove(row, col) {
  return row >= 0
         && row < this.ROWS
         && col >= 0
         && col < this.COLS
         && this.matrix[row][col] === 0;
}
```

Listing 10-5: mazeSolver.js

The cell must be within the maze bounds and should be part of a corridor.

We also provide a function to print the maze:

```
print() {
  for (let i = 0; i < this.ROWS; i++) {
    console.log(this.matrix[i].join(' '));
  }
}
```

Listing 10-6: mazeSolver.js

The following function implements the maze solving algorithm:

```
solve(row, col) {
  if (row === this.ROWS - 1 && col === this.COLS - 1) {
    this.stack.push(new Point(row, col));
    return 1;
  }

  if (this.canMove(row, col)) {
    this.stack.push(new Point(row, col));
    this.matrix[row][col] = 2; //Marking visited

    if (this.solve(row, col + 1) === 1) return 1; //Move right
    if (this.solve(row + 1, col) === 1) return 1; //Move down
    if (this.solve(row, col - 1) === 1) return 1; //Move left
    if (this.solve(row - 1, col) === 1) return 1; //Move up

    this.stack.pop(); //Backtrack
    return 0;
  }

  return 0;
}
```

Listing 10-7: mazeSolver.js

First of all, we check whether the destination has been reached by comparing the current row and column with the constant values ROWS and COLS.

In the opposite case, we first check if we can actually move to this cell, i.e., if it is part of a corridor and is within the maze bounds. If so, we add its coordinates into the stack and we mark the cell with the number 2, to mark the fact that we have already passed from this cell.

Then, we proceed with calling recursively the `solve()` function for all four directions, starting with right and down, and then trying with left and up. If none of those movements results in solving the maze (i.e. they all return 0), then we will have to backtrack. Since this point in the maze was not eventually part of the solution, we pop it from the stack.

We also define a function to print the path followed to solve the maze. We get it by popping the visited cells of the maze from the stack, one by one:

```
  printPath() {
    const path = [];
    while (!this.stack.isEmpty()) {
      const p = this.stack.pop();
      path.push(`(${p.row}, ${p.col})`);
    }
    console.log(path.reverse().join(', '));
  }
}
```

Listing 10-8: mazeSolver.js

Finally, let's see the main code of the program:

```
const maze = new Maze();

console.log('This is the maze:');
maze.print();

if (maze.solve(0, 0) === 1) {
  console.log('\n\nThis is the path found:');
  maze.printPath();

  console.log('\n\nThis is the maze with all the points crossed:');
  maze.print();
} else {
  console.log('No path found');
}
```

Listing 10-9: mazeSolver.js

We first print the initial maze, then we solve the maze and we print the solution path. Then we display the map once more; all the points that we crossed during our search will be marked with '2'.

You can run this code with Node.js:

```
node mazeSolver.js
```

You can find this project in GitHub:

https://github.com/htset/js_exercises_dsa/tree/master/MazeSolver

11. File Indexer

For this exercise, we will create a program that will recursively index all the files in a specified folder. The information about the indexed files (filename and location in the disk) will be stored in a *Binary Search Tree (BST)* for faster searching.

Proposed Solution

The Binary Search Tree structure is a tree where each node has only two children, left and right. Here is the definition of the class:

```
const fs = require('fs');
const path = require('path');

class Node {
  constructor(fileName, filePath) {
    this.fileName = fileName;
    this.filePath = filePath;
    this.left = null;
    this.right = null;
  }
}

class FileIndexer {
  constructor() {
    this.root = null;
  }

  ...
```

Listing 11-1: fileIndexer.js

Each node of the tree contains two strings, the filename and the file location. It also contains references to the two children nodes.

Next, we define a function to insert a new node into the tree:

```
//Insert node to tree
insertNode(fileName, filePath) {
  //If the tree is empty, insert node here
  if (this.root === null) {
    this.root = new Node(fileName, filePath);
    return;
  }

  //If not empty, then go down the tree
  let current = this.root;
  while (true) {
    if (fileName.localeCompare(current.fileName) < 0) {
      if (current.left === null) {
        current.left = new Node(fileName, filePath);
        return;
      }
```

```
      current = current.left;
    } else {
      if (current.right === null) {
        current.right = new Node(fileName, filePath);
        return;
      }
      current = current.right;
    }
  }
}
```

Listing 11-2: fileIndexer.js

Starting from the root of the tree, we move downwards to the left or to the right depending on the inserted value.

Next, we define the function that will recursively index all files into the tree:

```
//Index the specified directory
indexDirectoryHelper(dirPath) {
  //If it's not a directory, return
  if (!fs.existsSync(dirPath)) return;

  //loop over files or directories within directory
  const files = fs.readdirSync(dirPath);
  for (const file of files) {
    const filePath = path.join(dirPath, file);
    if (fs.lstatSync(filePath).isDirectory()) {
      //if it is a directory, then call indexDirectoryHelper() recursively
      this.indexDirectoryHelper(filePath);
    } else {
      //insert file in tree
      this.insertNode(file, filePath);
    }
  }
}
```

Listing 11-3: fileIndexer.js

We first check if a path exists and corresponds to a directory. We then loop over all the files and the directories inside the directory, one by one. If it is a file, then we insert it in the tree as new node. If it is a directory, then we recursively call `indexDirectoryHelper()`.

Next, we define a function to recursively delete the nodes of the tree:

```
deleteSubtree(root) {
  if (root !== null) {
    this.deleteSubtree(root.left);
    this.deleteSubtree(root.right);
    root = null;
  }
}
```

Listing 11-4: fileIndexer.js

We perform this by setting the root of the subtree to null, so that the subtree will be removed by the garbage collector.

Then, we have the directory traversal function (also recursive):

```
traverse(root) {
  if (root !== null) {
    this.traverse(root.left);
    console.log(`${root.fileName}: ${root.filePath}`);
    this.traverse(root.right);
  }
}
```

Listing 11-5: fileIndexer.js

Now, we define functions to index and print all the files in a directory. Those functions call the respective helper functions:

```
indexDirectory(directoryPath) {
  this.root = null;
  this.indexDirectoryHelper(directoryPath);
}

printFiles() {
  console.log('Indexed files:');
  this.traverse(this.root);
}
```

Listing 11-6: fileIndexer.js

After the tree has been set up, we can call function searchFileLocation() to get the location of a file:

```
searchFileLocation(filename) {
  let current = this.root;
  while (current !== null) {
    if (filename === current.fileName) {
      return current.filePath;
    } else if (filename.localeCompare(current.fileName) < 0) {
      current = current.left;
    } else {
      current = current.right;
    }
  }
  return '';
}
```

Listing 11-7: fileIndexer.js

We traverse the tree until we find a node with the specified file name. If the tree is exhausted, then we return null.

Finally, here is the main code of our program:

```
const readline = require('readline').createInterface({
  input: process.stdin,
  output: process.stdout
});

readline.question('Path to index recursively: ', (path) => {
  const indexer = new FileIndexer();
  indexer.indexDirectory(path);
  indexer.printFiles();

  readline.question("Let's search for a file's location. Give the file name: ",
  (filenameToSearch) => {
    const location = indexer.searchFileLocation(filenameToSearch);
    if (location) {
      console.log(`File ${filenameToSearch} found. Location: ${location}`);
    } else {
      console.log(`File ${filenameToSearch} not found.`);
    }
    readline.close();
  });
});
```

Listing 11-8: fileIndexer.js

Users can index the contents of a folder and then they can search for a specific filename.

You can run this code with Node.js:

`node fileIndexer.js`

You can find this project in GitHub:

https://github.com/htset/js_exercises_dsa/tree/master/FileIndexer

12. Inventory with AVL Tree

In this exercise, we will create an inventory program, that will store information about the company's products in an AVL tree structure.

Proposed Solution

An *AVL (Adelson-Velsky and Landis) tree* is a *self-balancing* binary search tree structure. By the term *balanced*, we mean that both branches of the tree have the same depth or differ by one level at the most. To achieve this, a process called *rebalancing* is occasionally performed, that changes the tree structure in way that the tree is closer to be balanced.

The AVL tree has almost the same structure as a simple binary search tree (BST); the difference lies in the rebalancing algorithm. Let's see the structure:

```
class Product {
  constructor(id, name, price, quantity) {
    this.id = id;
    this.name = name;
    this.price = price;
    this.quantity = quantity;
  }
}

class InventoryNode {
  constructor(product) {
    this.product = product;
    this.left = null;
    this.right = null;
    this.height = 1;
  }
}
```

Listing 12-1: inventoryAVL.js

The `InventoryNode` class contains a product object and two references to the tree's branches. Most importantly, it also contains the `height` property, which is used to track the tree's height.

Next, we define the `Inventory` class, which contains a reference that is the root of the AVL tree. We also define two internal functions of the tree:

```
class Inventory {
  constructor() {
    this.root = null;
  }

  getHeight(node) {
    return node === null ? 0 : node.height;
  }

  getBalance(node) {
```

```
    return node === null ? 0 : this.getHeight(node.left)-this.getHeight(node.right);
}
```
Listing 12-2: inventoryAVL.js

The former gives us the height of the tree, while the latter checks whether the tree is balanced or not.

Afterwards, we add code for the creation of a new node in the tree:

```
newNode(product) {
    return new InventoryNode(product);
}
```
Listing 12-3: inventoryAVL.js

Note that the height of the node is set to 1.

Next, we proceed with the definition of two functions for the rotation of the tree to the left or to the right:

```
rotateRight(y) {
    const x = y.left;
    const T2 = x.right;

    x.right = y;
    y.left = T2;

    y.height = Math.max(this.getHeight(y.left), this.getHeight(y.right)) + 1;
    x.height = Math.max(this.getHeight(x.left), this.getHeight(x.right)) + 1;

    return x;
}

rotateLeft(x) {
    const y = x.right;
    const T2 = y.left;

    y.left = x;
    x.right = T2;

    x.height = Math.max(this.getHeight(x.left), this.getHeight(x.right)) + 1;
    y.height = Math.max(this.getHeight(y.left), this.getHeight(y.right)) + 1;

    return y;
}
```
Listing 12-4: inventoryAVL.js

Those two functions will be used when we will try to insert a new node into the tree:

```
insertProduct(node, product) {
    if (node === null) return this.newNode(product);
```

```
    if (product.id < node.product.id) {
      node.left = this.insertProduct(node.left, product);
    } else if (product.id > node.product.id) {
      node.right = this.insertProduct(node.right, product);
    } else {
      return node;
    }

    node.height = 1 + Math.max(this.getHeight(node.left),
                               this.getHeight(node.right));

    const balance = this.getBalance(node);

    if (balance > 1 && product.id < node.left.product.id) {
      return this.rotateRight(node);
    }

    if (balance < -1 && product.id > node.right.product.id) {
      return this.rotateLeft(node);
    }

    if (balance > 1 && product.id > node.left.product.id) {
      node.left = this.rotateLeft(node.left);
      return this.rotateRight(node);
    }

    if (balance < -1 && product.id < node.right.product.id) {
      node.right = this.rotateRight(node.right);
      return this.rotateLeft(node);
    }

    return node;
  }
```

Listing 12-5: inventoryAVL.js

The idea here is to check for the tree balance after inserting a new node to it. If the tree becomes unbalanced, then we will have to rotate it either to the left or to the right.

Next, we present the functions to traverse the tree while printing its contents, as well as the code to search for a specific product in the tree:

```
  traverseTree(node) {
    if (node !== null) {
      this.traverseTree(node.left);
      console.log(`ID: ${node.product.id},
                   Name: ${node.product.name},
                   Price: ${node.product.price},
                   Quantity: ${node.product.quantity}`);
      this.traverseTree(node.right);
    }
  }
```

Listing 12-6: inventoryAVL.js

Traversing the tree means visiting each node in the tree, and this is performed recursively, first for the left branch and then for the right branch.

Searching for a product in the tree works in similar fashion: we visit a node, and we check the product's ID. If it matches the search ID, then we print the product details, and the function returns. Otherwise, we visit the left or the right branch of the tree recursively, depending on the search ID.

```js
searchProduct(node, id) {
  if (node === null || node.product.id === id) {
    if (node === null) {
      console.log('Product not found.');
    } else {
      console.log(`Found product: ID: ${node.product.id},
              Name: ${node.product.name},
              Price: ${node.product.price},
              Quantity: ${node.product.quantity}`);
    }
    return node;
  }

  console.log(`Visited product ID: ${node.product.id}`);

  if (id < node.product.id) {
    return this.searchProduct(node.left, id);
  } else {
    return this.searchProduct(node.right, id);
  }
}
```
Listing 12-7: inventoryAVL.js

All the functions we have defined so far are helper functions. We also define three functions that will call them:

```js
insertProductPublic(product) {
  this.root = this.insertProduct(this.root, product);
}

traverseTreePublic() {
  this.traverseTree(this.root);
}

searchProductPublic(id) {
  return this.searchProduct(this.root, id);
}
}
```
Listing 12-8: inventoryAVL.js

We use this convention because the respective helper functions with the same name (`insertProduct`, `traverseTree` and `searchProduct`) are called recursively. In this way, we provide a clean interface to programmers that will use our code.

Finally, here is the main code:

```
const inventory = new Inventory();
const products = Array.from({ length: 100 },
  (_, i) => new Product(i + 1, `Product ${i + 1}`,
    (Math.random() * 1000) / 10, Math.floor(Math.random() * 100) + 1));

//Shuffle products
for (let i = products.length - 1; i > 0; i--) {
  const j = Math.floor(Math.random() * (i + 1));
  [products[i], products[j]] = [products[j], products[i]];
}

//Insert products into inventory
for (const product of products) {
  inventory.insertProductPublic(product);
}

console.log('Inventory:');
inventory.traverseTreePublic();

const productIdToSearch = 35;
const foundProduct = inventory.searchProductPublic(productIdToSearch);

if (foundProduct !== null) {
  console.log(`Product found: ID: ${foundProduct.product.id},
            Name: ${foundProduct.product.name},
            Price: ${foundProduct.product.price},
            Quantity: ${foundProduct.product.quantity}`);
} else {
  console.log(`Product with ID ${productIdToSearch} not found.`);
}
```

Listing 12-9: inventoryAVL.js

We create 100 products with random quantities and prices and place them in an array. Then we shuffle the array in a random order. Afterwards, we insert the products into the AVL tree, and we print its contents.

Finally, a search is performed for a specific product ID. During the search process we print the visited nodes to get an idea of how fast we will find the specific ID inside the AVL tree.

You can run this code with Node.js:

```
node inventoryAVL.js
```

You can find this project in GitHub:

https://github.com/htset/js_exercises_dsa/tree/master/InventoryAVL

13. Social Network

A social network is essentially a *graph* of nodes that depicts the users of the network along with their connections to their friends. In this exercise, we will create such a graph and we will implement the functionality to recommend new friends according to a user's current connections.

Proposed Solution

There are various ways to implement the users' graph, for example using *sparse two-dimensional matrices*. Here we will construct the graph with the use of a *one-dimensional array* of users, where the connections are stored in a linked list:

```
class FriendNode {
  constructor(name) {
    this.name = name;
    this.next = null;
  }
}

class User {
  constructor(name) {
    this.name = name;
    this.friends = null;
  }
}
```

Listing 13-1: socialNetwork.js

The User class contains the name of the user as well as a linked list of the user's friends.

Next, we define a *queue* class that will be used by the friend recommendation algorithm:

```
class QueueNode {
  constructor(userIndex) {
    this.userIndex = userIndex;
    this.next = null;
  }
}

class Queue {
  constructor() {
    this.front = null;
    this.rear = null;
  }

  //Check if the queue is empty
  isEmpty() {
    return this.front === null;
  }

  //Add an element to the queue
  enqueue(userIndex) {
```

```
    const newNode = new QueueNode(userIndex);
    if (this.isEmpty()) {
      this.front = this.rear = newNode;
    } else {
      this.rear.next = newNode;
      this.rear = newNode;
    }
  }

  //Remove an element from the queue
  dequeue() {
    if (this.isEmpty()) {
      console.log("Queue is empty!");
      return -1;
    }

    const temp = this.front;
    const userIndex = temp.userIndex;
    this.front = this.front.next;

    if (this.front === null) {
      this.rear = null;
    }

    return userIndex;
  }
}
```
Listing 13-2: socialNetwork.js

The queue contains the indexes of the users, as they will appear inside the users' array (see below in the Graph class). We define the class for the queue nodes, and functions to enqueue and dequeue user indexes inside the queue, as well as to check whether it is empty or not.

Now, let's see how we will insert users into the graph and how we will define the connections with their friends. We define the Graph class, that essentially contains an array of all the users of the social network:

```
class Graph {
  constructor() {
    this.MAX_USERS = 100;
    this.users = [];
    this.numUsers = 0;
  }

  ...
```
Listing 13-3: socialNetwork.js

Next, we provide the functionality to add a new user to the graph:

```
  //Add a new user to the graph
  addUser(name) {
    if (this.numUsers >= this.MAX_USERS) {
```

```
    console.log("Max user limit reached!");
    return;
  }

  this.users.push(new User(name));
  this.numUsers++;
}
```
Listing 13-4: socialNetwork.js

We use the following function to add a new connection to a user:

```
//Add a connection (friendship) between two users
addConnection(src, dest) {
  if (src < 0 || src >= this.numUsers || dest < 0 || dest >= this.numUsers) {
    console.log("Invalid user index!");
    return;
  }

  const newFriendSrc = new FriendNode(this.users[dest].name);
  newFriendSrc.next = this.users[src].friends;
  this.users[src].friends = newFriendSrc;

  const newFriendDest = new FriendNode(this.users[src].name);
  newFriendDest.next = this.users[dest].friends;
  this.users[dest].friends = newFriendDest;
}
```
Listing 13-5: socialNetwork.js

Note that when we add a new connection, we make it bi-directional. That is, we insert a friend node for each one of the connection's ends.

Next, we proceed to the more interesting stuff, the recommender function:

```
//Recommend friends for a given user
recommendFriends(userIndex) {
  console.log(`Recommended friends for ${this.users[userIndex].name}:`);

  const queue = new Queue();
  const visited = Array(this.MAX_USERS).fill(0);

  visited[userIndex] = 1;
  queue.enqueue(userIndex);

  while (!queue.isEmpty()) {
    const currentUserIndex = queue.dequeue();
    let current = this.users[currentUserIndex].friends;

    while (current !== null) {
      let friendIndex = -1;
      for (let i = 0; i < this.numUsers; i++) {
        if (current.name === this.users[i].name) {
          friendIndex = i;
```

```
                break;
            }
        }

        if (friendIndex !== -1 && visited[friendIndex] === 0) {
            console.log(`- ${current.name}`);
            visited[friendIndex] = 1;
            queue.enqueue(friendIndex);
        }

        current = current.next;
      }
    }
  }
}
```

Listing 13-6: socialNetwork.js

As already mentioned, the algorithm makes use of a queue. In the queue, we store the indexes of the user's friends as we follow the linked list. We then use the queue to get the friends of the user's friends, and in this way, we can travel through the connections of the graph and find all the connected people to the specific user.

Note that we are using the `visited` array to store the persons that we have already visited. This will prevent the algorithm for looping to the same friends again and again and will ensure the convergence of our search.

Finally, here is the `main()` function:

```
function main() {
  const graph = new Graph();
  graph.addUser("User A");
  graph.addUser("User B");
  graph.addUser("User C");
  graph.addUser("User D");
  graph.addUser("User E");
  graph.addUser("User F");
  graph.addUser("User G");
  graph.addUser("User H");

  graph.addConnection(0, 1);
  graph.addConnection(1, 2);
  graph.addConnection(2, 3);
  graph.addConnection(4, 5);
  graph.addConnection(5, 7);
  graph.addConnection(3, 6);

  //Recommend friends for specified users
  graph.recommendFriends(0);
  graph.recommendFriends(1);
  graph.recommendFriends(7);
}
```

```
main();
```

Listing 13-7: socialNetwork.js

In `main()`, we add users to the graph and we enter their friend connections. Then we run the algorithm to get friend recommendations.

You can run this code with Node.js:

```
node socialNetwork.js
```

You can find this project in GitHub:

https://github.com/htset/js_exercises_dsa/tree/master/SocialNetwork

14. Flights

Let's create a console application that will maintain a list of flights between cities and that will find the best combination of flights in terms of ticket cost.

Proposed Solution

This problem involves creating a graph between the cities. This graph will be weighted, with the cost of the respective ticket. We will use *Dijkstra's algorithm* to find the cheapest path between two of those cities.

The solution will involve the use of priority queue. This time, we will use code from NPM:

https://www.npmjs.com/package/datastructures-js

We should first install the priority queue locally in our project:

`npm install @datastructures-js/priority-queue`

Now, we define the `City` struct that will store a map of the connected cities and the respective costs:

```
const { MinPriorityQueue } = require('@datastructures-js/priority-queue');
const readline = require('readline');

//Structure to represent each city
class City {
  constructor(name) {
    this.name = name;
    this.flights = new Map();
  }
}
```

Listing 14-1: flights.js

Next, we define the `FlightGraph` class:

```
//Graph class to represent all cities and flights
class FlightGraph {
  constructor() {
    //Map of city names and their objects
    this.cities = new Map();
  }

  ...
```

Listing 14-2: flights.js

This class contains all the cities objects in a map along with their names. We can add cities and flights to our graph with the following functions:

```
  //Add a city to the graph
```

```js
addCity(name) {
  this.cities.set(name, new City(name));
}

//Add a flight between two cities and its cost
addFlight(src, dest, cost) {
  //Assuming flights are bidirectional
  this.cities.get(src).flights.set(dest, cost);
  this.cities.get(dest).flights.set(src, cost);
}
```

Listing 14-3: flights.js

Note that we assume that flights are bidirectional, and that they have the same price in both directions.

Next, we calculate the cheapest route between two cities using Dijkstra's algorithm:

```js
//Function to find the cheapest route between two cities
//using Dijkstra's algorithm
findCheapestRoute(src, dest) {
  //Initialize the distance map and previous node map
  const dist = new Map();
  const prev = new Map();
  const pq = new MinPriorityQueue();

  //Set all distances to infinity initially
  for (const city of this.cities.keys()) {
    dist.set(city, Infinity);
    prev.set(city, null);
  }

  //Distance to the source is 0
  dist.set(src, 0);
  pq.enqueue({ element: src, priority: 0 });

  //Main loop to process each node
  while (!pq.isEmpty()) {
    const { element: u, priority: uDist } = pq.dequeue();

    //Process each neighbor of the current node
    for (const [v, cost] of this.cities.get(u).flights.entries()) {
      //If a shorter path to v is found
      if (dist.get(u) !== Infinity && dist.get(u) + cost < dist.get(v)) {
        dist.set(v, dist.get(u) + cost);
        prev.set(v, u);
        pq.enqueue({ element: v, priority: dist.get(v) });
      }
    }
  }

  //Reconstructing the path from source to destination
  const path = [];
  for (let at = dest; at !== null; at = prev.get(at)) {
```

```
      path.push(at);
    }
    path.reverse();

    return { path, totalPrice: dist.get(dest) };
  }
```
Listing 14-4: flights.js

Initially, we initialize a dictionary to store the distances from the source city to every other city, marking the source city's distance as 0 and all other cities as infinity. We use a priority queue to process cities based on their distance from the source, dequeuing the city with the shortest distance first.

For each dequeued city, we examine its neighboring cities, updating their distances if a shorter path through the current city is found. This process continues until all cities are visited or until the destination city is reached.

Upon completion, we reconstruct the shortest path from the source to the destination using the information stored in the previous node map, facilitating the determination of the total price of the route.

To avoid getting stuck in loops during the graph traversal, we keep track of the cities visited in the current path (`dist` map). If a city has already been visited in the current path, we skip exploring flights from that city to prevent loops.

We can calculate and print all the possible flights between two cities using *Depth-First Search (DFS)*:

```
//Display all possible flights between two cities using DFS
displayAllFlights(src, dest) {
  if (!this.cities.has(src) || !this.cities.has(dest)) {
    console.log('Invalid cities entered.');
    return;
  }

  const visited = new Set();
  const path = [];
  path.push(src);
  this.dfs(src, dest, visited, path);
}
```
Listing 14-5: flights.js

We see that function `displayAllFlights()` calls the recursive `dfs()` function:

```
//Recursive DFS function to find all flights between source and destination
dfs(src, dest, visited, path) {
  visited.add(src);

  if (src === dest) {
    this.printPath(path);
```

```
    } else {
      for (const flight of this.cities.get(src).flights.keys()) {
        if (!visited.has(flight)) {
          path.push(flight);
          this.dfs(flight, dest, visited, path);
          path.pop();
        }
      }
    }

    visited.delete(src);
  }
```
Listing 14-6: flights.js

The `dfs()` function in the `FlightGraph` class implements *Depth-First Search (DFS)* recursively to find all possible flights between a source and a destination city within a flight network.

It begins by marking the current city as visited and checks if it matches the destination city. If the destination is reached, it prints the current path. Otherwise, it explores all neighboring cities not yet visited by recursively calling itself for each neighbor.

During exploration, it pushes the neighboring city onto the `path` stack and continues the search until all possible paths from the current city are explored or until the destination is reached.

Upon backtracking, it removes the current city from the `path` stack and marks it as unvisited, allowing exploration of alternative paths. This process is repeated until all cities in the network are explored.

We use this stack to print the final path in `printPath()` function:

```
  //Helper function to print a path (array content)
  printPath(path) {
    console.log(path.join(' -> '));
  }
}
```
Listing 14-7: flights.js

Finally in the main code, we add cities and flights to the graph, and we ask the user to select a pair of cities to calculate the best (cheapest) combination of flights:

```
const graph = new FlightGraph();

graph.addCity("London");
graph.addCity("Paris");
graph.addCity("Berlin");
graph.addCity("Rome");
graph.addCity("Madrid");
graph.addCity("Amsterdam");
```

```
graph.addFlight("London", "Paris", 100);
graph.addFlight("London", "Berlin", 150);
graph.addFlight("London", "Madrid", 200);
graph.addFlight("Paris", "Berlin", 120);
graph.addFlight("Paris", "Rome", 180);
graph.addFlight("Berlin", "Rome", 220);
graph.addFlight("Madrid", "Rome", 250);
graph.addFlight("Madrid", "Amsterdam", 170);
graph.addFlight("Amsterdam", "Berlin", 130);

const rl = readline.createInterface({
  input: process.stdin,
  output: process.stdout
});

rl.question("Enter departure city: ", departure => {
  rl.question("Enter destination city: ", destination => {
    //Display all possible flights
    console.log(`All possible flights between ${departure} and ${destination}:`);
    graph.displayAllFlights(departure, destination);

    //Find the cheapest route and total price
    const { path, totalPrice } = graph.findCheapestRoute(departure, destination);

    //Display the cheapest route and total price
    console.log(`Cheapest Route: ${path.join(' -> ')}`);
    console.log(`Total Price: ${totalPrice}`);

    rl.close();
  });
});
```

Listing 14-8: flights.js

You can run this code with Node.js:

`node flights.js`

You can find this project in GitHub:

https://github.com/htset/js_exercises_dsa/tree/master/Flights

15. MNIST Image Comparison

In this exercise, we will play with handwriting images from the MNIST database.

Proposed Solution

The MNIST database (http://yann.lecun.com/exdb/mnist/) is a set of images depicting handwritten digits. The images are of 28x28 dimension and are typically used when studying pattern recognition and machine learning techniques.

Source: Wikipedia

We will download the following file and we will unzip it in our project's directory:

http://yann.lecun.com/exdb/mnist/train-images-idx3-ubyte.gz

We will also rename it as *input.dat*.

The first 15 bytes of this file, contain metadata about the images, i.e. the number of the images and their dimensions. Therefore, we will start reading from the 16th byte in steps of 28x28=784 bytes.

First, we define the `Image` class that will store the image data in a byte array:

```
const fs = require('fs');
const { promisify } = require('util');
const readFileAsync = promisify(fs.readFile);

class Image {
```

```javascript
  constructor(data, id) {
    this.data = new Uint8Array(data); //Using Uint8Array to mimic byte array behavior
    this.id = id;
  }

  print() {
    for (let i = 0; i < this.data.length; i++) {
      process.stdout.write(this.data[i] === 0 ? " " : "*");
      if ((i + 1) % 28 === 0) {
        process.stdout.write("\n");
      }
    }
  }

  euclideanDistance(img) {
    let distance = 0.0;
    for (let i = 0; i < this.data.length; i++) {
      distance += Math.sqrt(Math.pow((this.data[i] - img.data[i]), 2));
    }
    return Math.sqrt(distance);
  }
}
```

Listing 15-1: mnistImages.js

Inside the class, we implement the Image constructor and a function that prints the image as a series of asterisks.

We also implement the function that will calculate the *Euclidean distance* between two images, the current image and another one passed as function parameter. We are essentially calculating the sum of the differences between the respective bytes of two images. If the images are similar in content, then the distance will be minimized. Conversely, the distance will be higher, for images that have significant differences.

Now, let's see the main() function:

```javascript
async function main() {
  const ImageSize = 784;
  const MetaDataSize = 15;
  const images = [];

  try {
    const data = await readFileAsync('input.dat');
    let offset = MetaDataSize;

    while (offset < data.length) {
      const pixels = data.slice(offset, offset + ImageSize);
      images.push(new Image(pixels, images.length));
      offset += ImageSize;
    }
  } catch (err) {
    console.error('Error reading file:', err);
    return;
```

```
  }

  console.log(`Total images: ${images.length}`);

  //Example: Find the closest image to a randomly selected image
  const rand = () => Math.floor(Math.random() * images.length);

  //Generate a random index within the range of the list length
  const randomIndex = rand();
  console.log(`Random index: ${randomIndex}`);

  const randomImage = images[randomIndex];
  randomImage.print();

  let closestImage = null;
  let minDistance = Number.POSITIVE_INFINITY;
  let minIndex = 0;

  for (let i = 0; i < images.length; i++) {
    const distance = randomImage.euclideanDistance(images[i]);
    if (distance !== 0 && distance < minDistance) {
      minDistance = distance;
      minIndex = i;
      closestImage = images[i];
    }
  }

  //Output the label of the closest image
  console.log(`\nClosest image (distance=${minDistance}, index=${minIndex})\n`);

  //Print closest image
  closestImage.print();
}

main();
```

Listing 15-2: mnistImages.js

We use the `images` array to store the image references. After we open the *input.dat* binary file, we read it all in the `data` constant buffer. Then, in a loop, we read one image at a time (784 bytes) by slicing the data buffer and we add its reference to the respective `Image` object into the `images` array.

Afterwards, we get a randomly selected image from the list, and we print it using empty space where the byte is zero and an asterisk ('*') in places where the image bytes are non-zero. This way, we can get an idea of the handwriting digit that was chosen:

```
Total images: 60001
Random index: 48890




                    *******
                   ********
                   ********
                 ****** ***
                 **** ****
                ***** ***
                ****   ***
               *****  ****
               ****  ****   ***
              ****   ***   ****
              ****   *****  *****
              *****  **********
              ****************
               ***************
                ************
                   *******
                    ***
                    ****
                    ****
                     **
```

After printing the selected image, we iterate the images list, and we calculate the Euclidian distance between the randomly selected image and the currently selected image from the list. We maintain the minimum distance encountered and the corresponding image along with its ID.

At the end, we print the closest image that we got; it seems that the algorithm is working fine.

As a final note, this algorithm will take a lot of time to get the closest image, as it is checking all the images, one by one. There are other algorithms that will make this operation faster, albeit with a loss of precision.

One such example is the Locality-Sensitive Hashing[2] (LSH) algorithm, a technique used for approximate nearest neighbor search in high-dimensional spaces. LSH is particularly useful when dealing with large datasets where traditional exact nearest neighbor search functions become computationally expensive.

You can run this code with Node.js:

```
node mnistImages.js
```

Make sure you include the *input.dat* file in the same folder.

---

[2] https://en.wikipedia.org/wiki/Locality-sensitive_hashing

You can find this project in GitHub:

https://github.com/htset/js_exercises_dsa/tree/master/MNISTImages

16. HTTP Server with Caching

In this exercise, we will create a simple HTTP server that will serve static content (only HTML files). The web server will make use of a cache mechanism that will keep the most recently served content, in order to boost the server's performance.

Proposed Solution

The web server cache is a structure that stores the content that was previously sent to the client browser. The cache has limited space, so when it is filled up, we will need to empty the *least recently used (LRU)* entry in order to make space for the new entry. Moreover, when an entry is used by the server to send content to the client, then this entry is moved to the head of the list, as it is the more recently used entry.

Let's see the cache definition:

```
using System.Net;
using System.Net.Sockets;
using System.Text;

const net = require('net');
const fs = require('fs');

class LRUCache {
  constructor() {
    this.CACHE_SIZE = 3;
    this.head = null;
    this.tail = null;
    this.size = 0;
  }

  ...
```

Listing 16-1: webServerCache.js

The cache is implemented as a *doubly linked list*. In this kind of linked list, we can move to both directions, forward and backward. The doubly linked list is beneficial in our case as we can efficiently remove and insert nodes anywhere in the list without needing to traverse the list from the beginning. The same effect could be achieved with simple linked lists, or even arrays, but with lower performance.

Let's skip the rest of the cache definition for now, and jump to the main part of our program:

```
const server = new HttpServer();
server.start();
```

Listing 16-2: webServerCache.js

Here, we create an object of the `HttpServer` class, that will handle the connections with the clients. Let's see how it is implemented:

```javascript
class HttpServer {
  constructor() {
    this.PORT = 8080;
    this.MAX_REQUEST_SIZE = 1024;
    this.cache = new LRUCache();
  }

  start() {
    const server = net.createServer((client) => {
      console.log("Client connected.");

      client.on('data', (data) => {
        const request = data.toString('utf-8');
        console.log("Received request: " + request);

        //Find request type (GET)
        const parts = request.split(' ');
        if (parts.length < 2 || parts[0] !== "GET") {
          console.log("Invalid request format.");
          return;
        }

        //Get request url and check whether it is already stored in the cache
        const url = parts[1];
        let content = this.cache.getContent(url);

        if (content === "") {
          try {
            //If not found in cache, read it from the HTML file
            //We assume the files are in the same directory as the executable
            content = fs.readFileSync(url.substring(1), 'utf-8');
            console.log("Got content from file: " + content);
            this.cache.putContent(url, content);
          } catch (error) {
            console.log("File not found: " + url.substring(1));
            content = "HTTP/1.1 404 Not Found\r\n\r\n";
          }
        } else {
          console.log("Serving content from cache.");
        }

        //Check if the content is HTML or plain text
        let contentType = "text/plain"; //Default content type is plain text
        if (url.endsWith(".html") || url.endsWith(".htm")) {
          //If the URL ends with .html or .htm, it's HTML content
          contentType = "text/html";
        }

        //Build the response
        const response = "HTTP/1.1 200 OK\r\nContent-Type: "
          + contentType + "\r\n\r\n" + content;
        client.write(response);
        client.end();
      });
    });
```

```
    client.on('end', () => {
      console.log("Client disconnected.");
    });

    client.on('error', (error) => {
      console.error("Error with client:", error);
    });
  });

  server.listen(this.PORT, () => {
    console.log("Server started on port " + this.PORT);
  });
 }
}
```
Listing 16-3: webServerCache.js

Here we create a server object that waits for HTTP connections from web browsers at port 8080. When the server receives a request, then the `on('data')` handler function is called.

Initially, the web request is received into the `request` string. The string is split to retrieve the request type and the URL; only GET requests are handled by our server.

We then use the request URL to search in the cache for a previously stored response for this URL. If such an entry is not found in the cache, then we open the requested HTML file (The HTML files are stored in the same folder as our executable), and we transmit its HTML content in the response. Note that, before sending the content, we must send the header of the response:

`HTTP/1.1 200 OK\nContent-Type: text/html`

If the URL is found in the cache, then we get the content from there and we send it with the response.

Let's see how we do this, in function `getContent()` from the `LRUCache` class:

```
//Get the content associated with a URL from the cache
getContent(url) {
  let current = this.head;
  while (current !== null) {
    if (current.url === url) {
      this.moveToHead(current);
      console.log("Got content from cache: " + current.content);
      return current.content;
    }
    current = current.next;
  }
  return "";
}
```

Listing 16-4: webServerCache.js

We start from the head of the list, and we search for the URL in the cache's nodes. If we find the URL, then we move the node to the head of the cache (the *most recently used entry*) and we return the stored HTML content. The function returns an empty string if the URL is not found in the cache.

When a page is read from its file, then we store its content into the cache, with putContent():

```
//Put a URL-content pair into the cache
putContent(url, content) {
  if (this.size === this.CACHE_SIZE) {
    this.deleteNode(this.tail);
    this.size--;
  }
  const newNode = this.createNode(url, content);
  this.insertAtHead(newNode);
  this.size++;
}
```

Listing 16-5: webServerCache.js

If we have reached the maximum cache size, then the *LRU algorithm* kicks in: we delete the least recently used entry (the node at the tail of the list) and we make space for the insertion of the new entry (at the head of the list).

Now we can examine the functions that handle the cache operations. First, let's see how we can create a new node:

```
//Create a new node
createNode(url, content) {
  const newNode = {
    url: url,
    content: content,
    prev: null,
    next: null
  };
  console.log("New node created: " + content);
  return newNode;
}
```

Listing 16-6: webServerCache.js

Next, we see how to insert a new node at the head of the cache:

```
//Insert a new node at the head of the cache
insertAtHead(node) {
  node.next = this.head;
  node.prev = null;
  if (this.head !== null)
    this.head.prev = node;
  this.head = node;
```

```js
    if (this.tail === null)
      this.tail = node;
    console.log("Node inserted at head: " + node.content);
  }
```

Listing 16-7: webServerCache.js

Note that in all operations we must take care of all four references: head, tail, next, prev.

As part of the LRU algorithm, we have to move a node to the head of the list:

```js
  //Move a node to the head of the cache
  moveToHead(node) {
    if (node === this.head)
      return;
    if (node.prev !== null)
      node.prev.next = node.next;
    if (node.next !== null)
      node.next.prev = node.prev;
    node.prev = null;
    node.next = this.head;
    if (this.head !== null)
      this.head.prev = node;
    this.head = node;
    if (this.tail === null)
      this.tail = node;
    console.log("Node moved to head: " + node.content);
  }
```

Listing 16-8: webServerCache.js

Finally, here is the code for node deletion:

```js
  //Delete a node from the cache
  deleteNode(node) {
    if (node === null)
      return;
    if (node === this.head)
      this.head = node.next;
    if (node === this.tail)
      this.tail = node.prev;
    if (node.prev !== null)
      node.prev.next = node.next;
    if (node.next !== null)
      node.next.prev = node.prev;
    console.log("Node deleted: " + node.content);
  }
}
```

Listing 16-9: webServerCache.js

You can run the web server with Node.js:

```
node webServerCache.js
```

Then, you can open the main web page (http://localhost:8080/index.html) in a browser. Don't forget to add the sample HTML files included in the project in GitHub.

You can find this project in GitHub:

https://github.com/htset/js_exercises_dsa/tree/master/WebServerCache

17. Auction

In this exercise, we will create an auction process, that will consist of an auction server that receives bids from multiple clients. The clients will communicate with the server via web sockets. The server will wait for 20 seconds (using a timer) for a new bid, or else the auction is over and the maximum bid wins. The timer will be reset upon timely submission of new bid.

Proposed Solution

Let's start with the auction server. We will create an HTTP server that will listen to port 8080:

```js
const WebSocket = require('ws');
const http = require('http');
const fs = require('fs');

const PORT = 8080;
let clients = [];
let bestBid = 0;
let winningClient = null;
let auctionTimeout;

//Create an HTTP server
const html = fs.readFileSync('./index.html');

const server = http.createServer(function (request, response) {
  response.writeHead(200, { "Content-Type": "text/html" });
  response.write(html);
  response.end();
}).listen(PORT, () => {
  console.log(`Server listening on port ${PORT}`);
  resetAuctionTimeout();
});
```

Listing 17-1: server.js

We also create a web socket server:

```js
//Create a WebSocket server
const wss = new WebSocket.Server({ server });

//Handle new WebSocket connections
wss.on('connection', (ws) => {
  clients.push(ws);
  const clientId = clients.length;
  console.log(`Client no. ${clientId + 1} connected.`);
  handleConnection(ws, clientId);
});
```

Listing 17-2: server.js

When a new web socket connection arrives at the server, the connection event is fired. We then push the new client into an array of clients and we handle the connection in handleConnection():

```js
//Function to handle new client connection
function handleConnection(ws, clientId) {
  ws.on('message', (message) => {
    const bidAmount = parseInt(message, 10);
    console.log(`Received bid ${bidAmount} from client ${clientId}`);

    if (bidAmount > bestBid) {
      bestBid = bidAmount;
      winningClient = clientId;
      const msg = `New best bid: ${bestBid} (Client: ${winningClient})`;
      broadcast(msg);
      console.log(msg);
      resetAuctionTimeout();
    } else {
      const msg = `Received lower bid. Best bid remains at: ${bestBid}`;
      ws.send(msg);
      console.log(msg);
    }
  });

  ws.on('close', () => {
    console.log(`Client disconnected: ${clientId}`);
    clients[clientId] = null;
  });
}
```
Listing 17-3: server.js

This function essentially defines two handler functions for the message and close events. When a new message arrives, the bid amount is parsed. If the client has actually sent a valid bid, we compare it with the current maximum bid and we update this value if we got a higher bid. We also proceed with informing all clients about the submitted bid with broadcast() function. We also reset the timer to get a new 20 seconds' period with resetAuctionTimeout().

Here is the code for broadcast():

```js
//Function to broadcast a message to all connected clients
function broadcast(message) {
  clients.forEach((client) => {
    if (client) {
      client.send(message);
    }
  });
}
```
Listing 17-4: server.js

And here is the code for ending an auction as well as resetting the auction timeout:

```
//Function to end the auction
function endAuction() {
  const msg = `Auction finished. Winning bid: ${bestBid},
              winner: client no. ${winningClient}`;
  broadcast(msg);
  console.log(msg);
  process.exit(0);
}

//Function to reset the auction timeout
function resetAuctionTimeout() {
  if (auctionTimeout) {
    clearTimeout(auctionTimeout);
  }
  auctionTimeout = setTimeout(endAuction, 20000);
}
```

Listing 17-5: server.js

The users that take part in the auction will have to load the *index.html* file from localhost. Here is the code:

```
<!DOCTYPE html>
<html lang="en">
<head>
  <meta charset="UTF-8">
  <title>Auction Client</title>
</head>
<body>
  <h1>Auction Client</h1>
  <input type="number" id="bidAmount" placeholder="Enter your bid">
  <button onclick="sendBid()">Send Bid</button>
  <div id="messages"></div>

  <script>
    const ws = new WebSocket('ws://localhost:8080');

    ws.onmessage = (event) => {
      const messagesDiv = document.getElementById('messages');
      messagesDiv.innerHTML += `<p>${event.data}</p>`;
    };

    function sendBid() {
      const bidAmount = document.getElementById('bidAmount').value;
      ws.send(bidAmount);
    }
  </script>
</body>
</html>
```

Listing 17-6: index.html

When this HTML page is loaded, it connects via web sockets to the server. When the user submits a new bid, then sendBid() is called, and sends a message with send(). When a message is received from the server, the `onmessage` event handler is called, and displays the message on the user's page.

To run this project, you will need to first run the server:

`Node server.js`

Then, you will need to open the client web page from http://localhost:8080/index.html

You can find this project in GitHub:

https://github.com/htset/js_exercises_dsa/tree/master/Auction

www.ingramcontent.com/pod-product-compliance
Lightning Source LLC
Chambersburg PA
CBHW082238220526
45479CB00005B/1270